My Very First Bible

Retold By **L.J. SATTGAST**

Illustrated By **RUSS FLINT**

HARVEST HOUSE PUBLISHING
Eugene, Oregon 97402

For Caleb and Allison

MY VERY FIRST BIBLE
New Testament Stories for Young Children

Library of Congress Cataloging-in-Publication Data

Sattgast, L.J.
    My very first Bible: New Testament stories for young children /
retold by L.J. Sattgast; illustrated by Russ Flint.
        p.   cm.
    Summary: An illustrated collection of forty-nine Bible
stories from the New Testament.
    ISBN 0-89081-756-1
    1. Bible stories, English—N.T.   [1. Bible stories—N.T.]
I. Flint, Russ, ill.   II. Bible. N.T. Selections. 1989. III. Title.
BS2401.S28   1989
225.9'505—dc20   89-31534
                                                            CIP
                                                            AC

Copyright © 1989 by Harvest House Publishers
Eugene, Oregon 97402

Printed in the United States of America.

Presented to

_____

From

_____

On

_____

Contents

7   A New Baby

18   Where Is The King?

22   The Missing Boy

27   Jesus And The Dove

31   The Hard Test

32   A Happy Wedding

36   Jesus And The People

40   Nicodemus Learns A Lesson

43   An Important Decision

50   The Mountainside Talk

53   The Paralyzed Man

58   The Wind Obeys

62   A Girl And A Lady

66   Two Good Hands

70   A Bagful Of Seeds

72   A Boy's Lunch

77   Peter Gets Wet

81   Who Am I?

84   A Boy Is Helped

87   The Good Neighbor

91   One Is Thankful

95   Lost And Found

103   Jesus Loves Children

106   The Day Jesus Cried

110	Me First!	176	They Told A Lie
113	Little Man In A Tree	180	A Ride In The Chariot
119	A Blind Man Sees	183	The Light On The Road
123	Jesus Rides A Donkey	189	The Widows' Friend
130	Two Small Coins	193	God Loves Everybody
132	Money For Judas	198	Peter And The Angel
136	The Last Meal	201	A Long Journey
140	The Garden	204	It Happened In Philippi
148	The Sad Day	209	Two Cities
154	The Happy Day	212	Paul In Prison
160	Jesus Says Goodbye	216	The Shipwreck
166	The New Helper	220	Heaven Is Our Home
171	The Beggar Jumps		

A New Baby

Matthew 1; Luke 1, 2

Tucked away on a hillside, in the land of Israel, was a little town called Nazareth. A young woman named Mary lived there with her father and mother.

One day God sent an angel named Gabriel to talk with Mary.

At first Mary was afraid, but Gabriel said, "Don't be afraid! I came to tell you that God is pleased with you. He has chosen you to be the mother of his Son, Jesus, who will be a great King."

"I am happy to do what God wants," replied Mary.

Nearby lived a good man named Joseph. He would soon become Mary's husband.

Joseph was a carpenter. He used his tools to make tables and chairs out of wood. See how hard he works!

One night an angel appeared to Joseph in a dream. The angel told him about the special baby that Mary was going to have.

"You must call his name Jesus," said the angel, "for he will save people from their sins."

Soon after they were married, Joseph and Mary traveled to the town of Bethlehem.

Mary rode on the donkey while Joseph walked ahead leading the way.

When they reached Bethlehem, Mary and Joseph were very tired. But Bethlehem was crowded with many other visitors.

"Please, sir," said Joseph to the innkeeper, "do you have a room for tired travelers?"

"Every room is filled," replied the innkeeper, "but you may stay in the stable if you wish."

There in the stable, surrounded by curious animals, little baby Jesus was born. His mother, Mary, wrapped him up in a warm cloth and laid him in a manger filled with sweet-smelling hay.

Not far away, in a field, some shepherds were taking care of their sheep. It was a peaceful night and all was quiet.

Suddenly a bright angel appeared!

The shepherds were frightened, but the angel said, "Don't be afraid! I have good news for you! Today a baby was born who is the Savior of the world. You can find him in Bethlehem. He is all wrapped up in a warm cloth, lying in a manger."

Then the whole sky was filled with angels singing praises to God!

When the angels disappeared, the shepherds hurried
to Bethlehem to look for the baby. They found Mary and
Joseph and baby Jesus just as the angels had said.

The shepherds were so excited that they told everyone
they met about Jesus!

Where Is The King?

Matthew 2:1–12

One night, far away from Bethlehem, a bright new star appeared in the sky.

"What a magnificent star!" exclaimed some wise men who were watching it carefully. They decided to follow the star, for they were certain it would lead them to a great King.

"Where is the new King?" they asked when they came to Jerusalem. But King Herod had not heard about the baby, and he was not happy to hear about another king who might take his place.

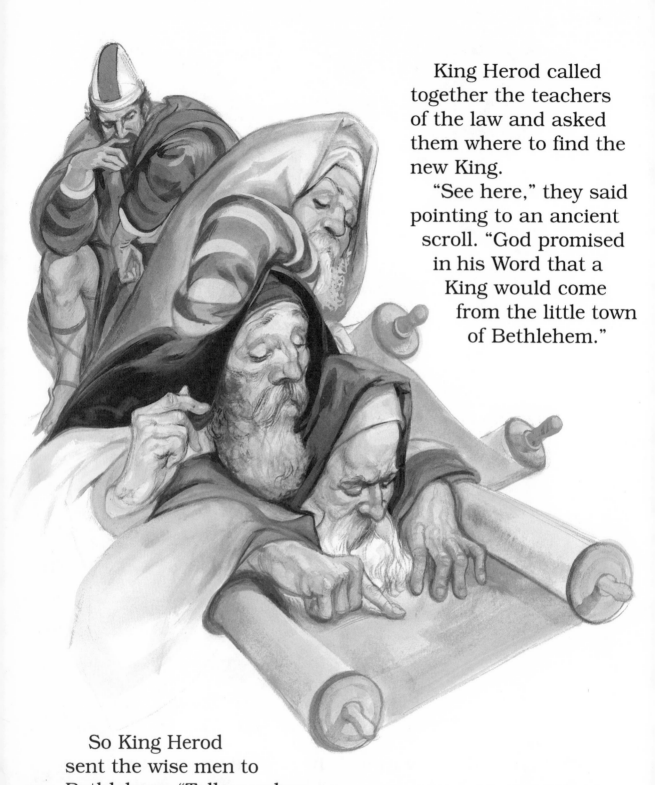

King Herod called together the teachers of the law and asked them where to find the new King.

"See here," they said pointing to an ancient scroll. "God promised in his Word that a King would come from the little town of Bethlehem."

So King Herod sent the wise men to Bethlehem. "Tell me when you find the baby so I can visit him too," he told them.

Do you think King Herod really wanted to visit the baby? No, he did not! He wanted to get rid of the new King!

The wise men followed the star to Joseph and Mary's house in Bethlehem.

When they saw Jesus, they bowed down and gave him wonderful gifts of gold, frankincense, and myrrh.
They did not tell King Herod about Jesus because God told them not to. God was taking care of little Jesus!

The Missing Boy

Luke 2:41–52

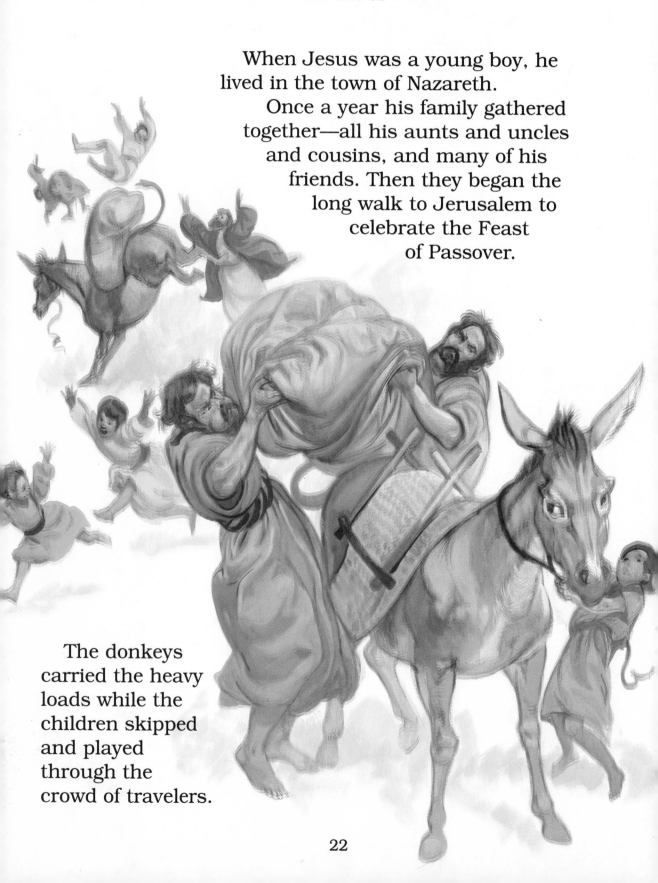

When Jesus was a young boy, he lived in the town of Nazareth.

Once a year his family gathered together—all his aunts and uncles and cousins, and many of his friends. Then they began the long walk to Jerusalem to celebrate the Feast of Passover.

The donkeys carried the heavy loads while the children skipped and played through the crowd of travelers.

The Feast of Passover was a wonderful holiday
for Jesus. He would eat a special meal and hear the
story of how God had saved his great, great, great
grandparents from a wicked king named Pharaoh.

Jesus loved to go to Jerusalem. He especially loved to see the temple where people went to pray and worship God. When it was time to go back home, Jesus slipped away to visit the temple one more time.

Mary and Joseph didn't miss Jesus until they had left Jerusalem and walked a long way.

"Have you seen Jesus?" they asked one person after another.

"No, we have not," everyone answered.

So Mary and Joseph went back to Jerusalem looking for Jesus. After three days they found him in the temple talking with the teachers. The teachers were very surprised that a young boy knew so much about God's Word!

Mary ran over to Jesus. "Son! Why have you worried us like this? We have been looking everywhere for you!"

"Didn't you know I would be here in my Father's house?" asked Jesus. He knew that God was his real Father.

So Jesus returned home with Mary and Joseph. As he grew up he was loved by God and by all who knew him.

Jesus And The Dove

Matthew 3:1–17

Many years later, after Jesus had grown into a man, he went to see his cousin John. John was a strange-looking man. He did not dress or eat like other people. But he had something very important to say.

"You must feel sorry for your sins," he said, "and stop doing what is wrong!"

One by one the people confessed their sins.
"We are sorry for disobeying God," they said sadly.
Then down into the river they went to be baptized
by John. This showed everyone that they wanted to
live for God and do what was right.

"I want to be baptized too," said Jesus.

"Oh, no!" replied John. "You have never done anything wrong. I don't need to baptize you!"

But Jesus replied, "It is important for me to do what is right." So John baptized him there in the river.

When Jesus came out of the water, the sky
opened up and God's Spirit came down in the shape
of a beautiful dove. As it landed gently on Jesus they
heard God say, "You are my Son and I love you!"

The Hard Test

Matthew 4:1–11

Someone is bothering Jesus. Do you know who it is? It is Satan! Satan is always fighting against God. He tried to get Jesus to disobey God.

Do you know what Jesus did? He remembered Bible verses he had learned, and said them out loud. Satan did not like to hear God's Word, so he went away and left Jesus alone. Here is a verse from the Bible that you can learn:

I have hidden your word in my heart that I might not sin against you.
Psalm 119:11 NIV

A Happy Wedding

John 2:1–11

One day Jesus and his friends were invited to a wedding. Mary, the mother of Jesus, went too.

See how happy everyone is! People are talking and laughing, and there is plenty to eat and drink.

But then something terrible happened.

"Look!" said Mary to Jesus. "They ran out of wine! Now what will all the people drink?"

Mary knew that Jesus could help, so she went over to the servants. "See that man over there?" she said, pointing to Jesus. "Do whatever he tells you to do!"

Nearby there were six empty water jars. "Fill those jars with water," Jesus told the servants. So they filled them up to the very top.

"Now pour some out and take it to the master in charge of the food," Jesus commanded.

The servants did as Jesus said, and filled a glass for the master. But now it was no longer water! Jesus had turned the water into wine. It was a miracle!

"What good-tasting wine!" said the master in charge of the food. He did not realize what Jesus had done. But the servants who poured the water knew.

This was the first miracle that Jesus ever did. It showed his friends who he really was—God's Son.

Jesus And The People

Matthew 4:12–17
Luke 4:38–44

Herod was a very bad king. He did many terrible things. "Stop doing what is wrong!" said John the Baptist to the king one day. This made Herod very angry. So he put John in prison. What a wicked king he was!

When Jesus heard that his cousin John was in prison, he began to travel from town to town telling people about God.

One day he stayed in the home of his friend Peter.

Peter's mother-in-law was very sick, so Jesus bent down over her bed and told the sickness to go away. She got well immediately and began to fix food for everyone!

Then people began bringing their sick friends to Jesus. He touched each one and made them well.

"Won't you stay here with us?" the people begged.

"No," he replied, "I must also go to other towns and tell them the good news about God."

Nicodemus Learns A Lesson

John 3:1–16

It was nighttime in the city of Jerusalem. Outside it was dark, and the wind whistled and blew through the narrow, crooked streets.

Most people were nice and warm in their snug houses, but not Nicodemus. He hurried along in the dark all alone, for he did not want anyone to know he was going to see Jesus.

Soon Nicodemus was talking with Jesus. "Teacher," he said, "you must have come from God, for only God can do miracles."

In reply Jesus said, "Nicodemus, if you want to see God someday, you must be born again. The first time you were born, you were a little baby. But when you are born again, God's Holy Spirit comes to live inside you."

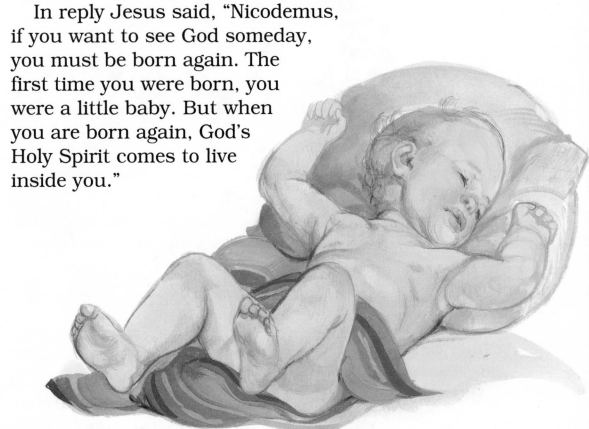

"I don't understand," said Nicodemus.

"God's Spirit is like the wind," explained Jesus. "You can't see the wind, but you can feel it blowing. You can't see God's Spirit either, but he helps us to obey God."

Jesus talked with Nicodemus a long time. He told him how much God loves everyone in the whole wide world!

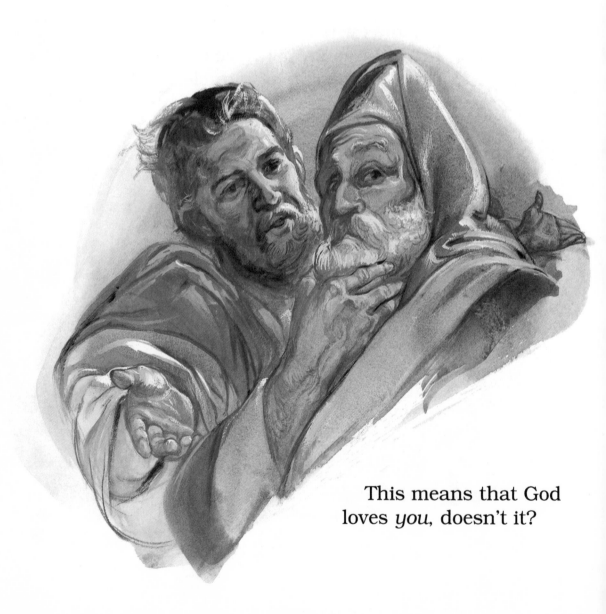

This means that God loves *you*, doesn't it?

An Important Decision

Luke 6:12–16

Jesus had many friends called disciples. His disciples listened to him and believed what he said. They often followed him as he walked from one town to another telling people about God.

Peter and his brother Andrew were fishermen. They left their fishing nets behind and followed Jesus.

Mary Magdalene had been sick, but Jesus made her well. She helped buy food for Jesus and his disciples when they traveled.

Matthew collected tax money from people. But when he met Jesus, he left the money behind on the table and followed him.

Mary and Martha and their brother Lazarus were disciples too. When Jesus came to the village of Bethany, he often stayed in their home.

But now Jesus was going to choose twelve disciples to be his special friends. They would stay together and he would teach them many things.

Jesus walked up into the hills to pray. He wanted to talk to God about this important decision.

Soon it grew dark, but Jesus did not go home. One by one the stars came out, but still Jesus prayed. All night long he talked with God.

When the sun came up the next morning, Jesus was ready. He called all the disciples together, and this is who he picked:

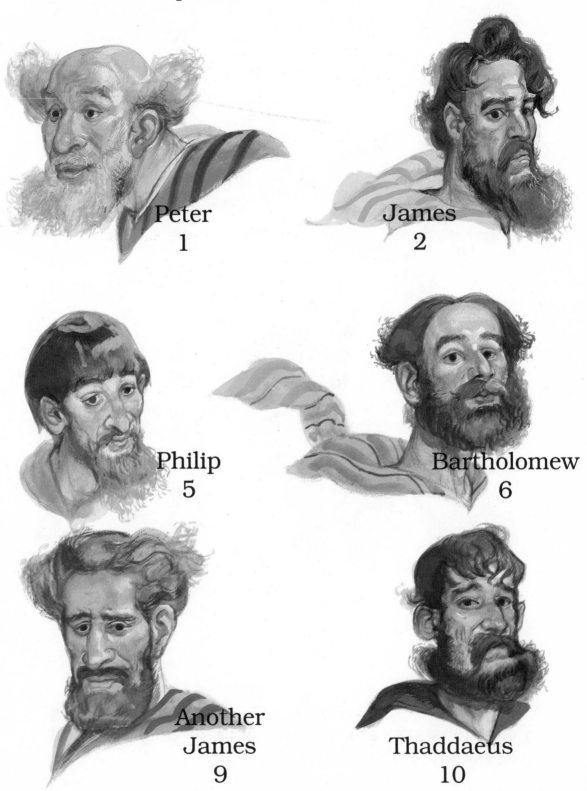

Peter
1

James
2

Philip
5

Bartholomew
6

Another
James
9

Thaddaeus
10

Can you count them?

John
3

Andrew
4

Matthew
7

Thomas
8

Simon
11

Judas
Iscariot
12

The Mountainside Talk

Matthew 5, 6, 7

Look at all the people! Can you find Jesus?
He is sitting on the mountainside talking while
everyone listens. This is what he is saying:

You are like a lamp shining brightly when you are good. Other people can see that you love God.

God is kind to everyone by sending the sunshine and the rain. We should be kind to everyone too.

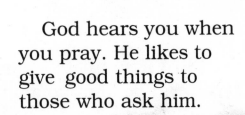

God takes care of the birds and the flowers, and he will take care of you too.

God hears you when you pray. He likes to give good things to those who ask him.

Then Jesus said, "If you listen to me and do what I say, you will be like the wise man who built his house on the rock. See? Even the waves can't knock down his house!"

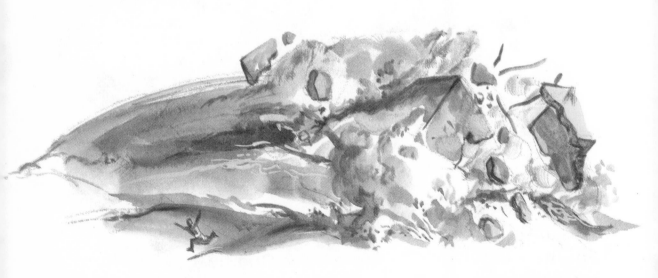

"But if you listen to me and do not do what I say, you will be like the foolish man who built his house on the sand. Crash! went the house. It has fallen to pieces! How important it is to obey God!"

The Paralyzed Man

Mark 2:1–12

In Capernaum there lived a paralyzed man. He could not move his legs. He could not walk around. All day long he lay on his mat while other people took care of him.

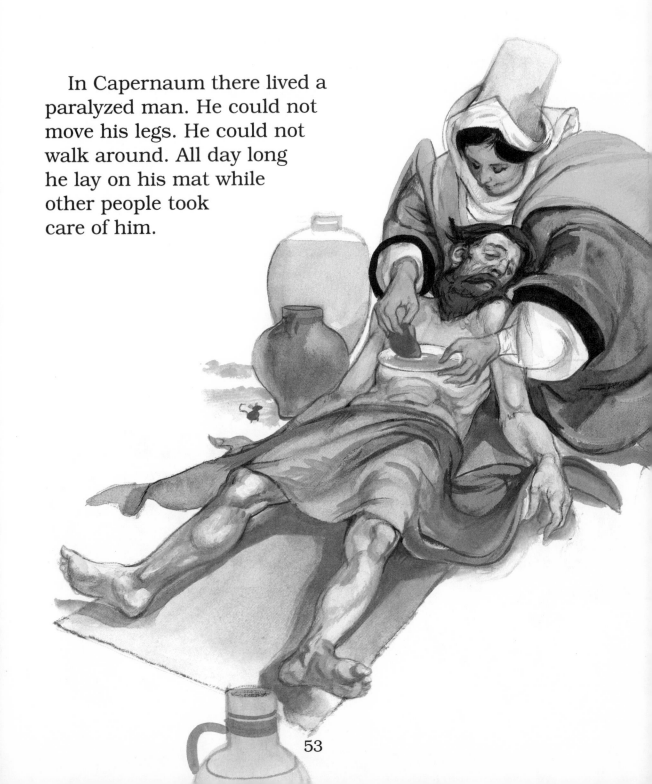

One day Jesus visited Capernaum. "Perhaps Jesus can heal me," thought the paralyzed man.

So his friends carried him on his mat to see Jesus. But there were so many people that they could not even get in the door.

"What shall we do?" cried the paralyzed man.

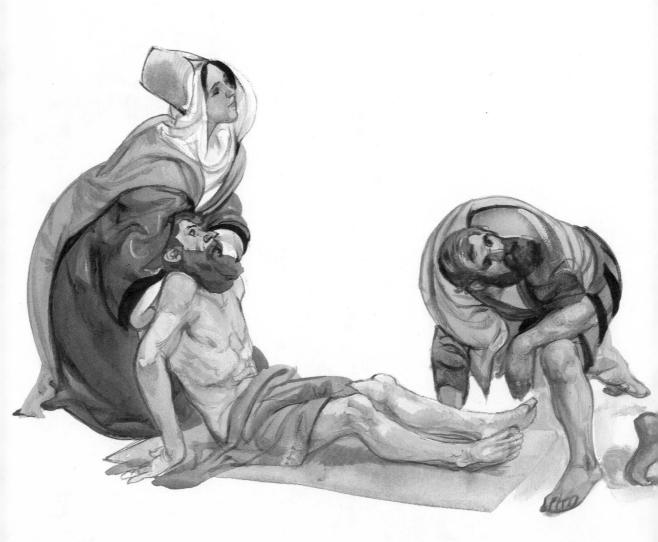

"We will climb up on the roof," decided his four friends, "and make a hole big enough to let you down right in front of Jesus!"

And so they did.

When Jesus saw the paralyzed man, he said, "Friend, I forgive your sins!"

Some men standing nearby did not like what Jesus said. "Only God can forgive sins," they thought.

But Jesus knew what they were thinking.

"To show you I can forgive sins," he said, "I will also heal this man." Turning to the paralyzed man he said, "Get up, pick up your mat, and go home!"

The paralyzed man stood up. He began to walk! Everyone praised God and said, "We have seen a wonderful miracle today!"

The Wind Obeys

Mark 4:35–41

One evening after talking with people all day long, Jesus was tired. "Let's go to the other side of the lake," he said to his disciples. So they got into a boat and soon were far away from the crowd. Jesus laid his head on a pillow and fell fast asleep in the back of the boat.

Suddenly a storm came up. The waves were so high that they splashed over the top of the boat. "Jesus! Wake up!" cried his disciples. "Don't you care if the boat sinks?"

Jesus got
up and spoke
to the storm.
"Be quiet!"
he said. "Calm
down!"

Immediately the wind stopped and the water was still.

"Why were you so afraid?" said Jesus. "Why didn't you trust in God?"

His disciples didn't know what to think. "Even the wind and the waves obey him!" they whispered.

A Girl
And A Lady

Mark 5:21–43

This man's name
is Jairus. He has
only one daughter,
and he loves her
very much.

One day Jairus' little girl got very sick. He was
afraid she would not get well. So Jairus went to
look for Jesus.

When Jairus found Jesus he fell down at his feet. "Please come and make my daughter well again," he begged. So Jesus went with Jairus.

Now there was a woman in the crowd who had been sick for a long time.

"If I can just touch Jesus' clothes I will get well!" she thought. So she reached out and touched his robe. Right away she felt better.

Jesus knew what had happened. "Who touched me?" he asked. The woman was afraid and fell down at Jesus' feet.

"I did!" she confessed.

Jesus looked at her kindly. "Daughter," he said, "your faith has made you well."

Just then some men came from Jairus' house. "Your little girl has died," they told him, "so don't bother Jesus anymore." But Jesus said, "Don't be afraid!" and he kept on walking.

When they reached the house, Jesus took the girl by the hand and said, "Little girl, get up!"

How happy her mother and father were when they saw her stand right up and walk around!

Two Good Hands

Mark 3:1–6

There was one very important rule in the land of Israel. And this was the rule: You must not do any work on Saturday. Instead, you are to rest and worship God.

So every Saturday the people met to worship God. Jesus went too, and he often taught the lesson. The other teachers didn't like Jesus because the people listened to him instead of paying attention to them.

One Saturday while Jesus was teaching, he noticed a man with a shriveled hand. The teachers were watching Jesus closely to see what he would do. "If he heals this man," they thought, "he will be disobeying God, for God told us not to work on Saturday."

Jesus knew what they were thinking. He told the man with the shriveled hand, to stand up in front of everyone. "Does God want us to do good on Saturday?" he asked the teachers. "Yes, he does!"

Then Jesus said to the man, "Stretch out your hand!" Immediately the man's hand was healed. Now he had two good hands! But the teachers were very angry. They began to plot how they could get rid of Jesus.

A Bagful Of Seeds

Matthew 13:1–23

Jesus sat down by the lake one day. A large crowd of people came to hear him talk. So he sat in a boat where they could see him and told them this story:

The farmer gets up early and goes out to his field. He carries his bag of seed on his shoulder. The farmer tosses the seed here and there.

Some of the seeds fall on the path. The birds eat them.

Some of the seeds fall on the rocks. There is not enough dirt for them to grow.

Some of the seeds fall in a thornbush. There is not enough room for them to grow.

But some of the seeds fall on good ground. They grow and grow into tall, beautiful plants.

God's Word is like the seed, and we are like the good ground when we listen to God's Word and obey it.

The Little Boy's Lunch

John 6:1–13

Jesus and the twelve disciples were tired. For many days they had been teaching and healing sick people.

"Let's find a place to be alone," said Jesus. So they got into a boat and sailed to the other side of the lake.

But when they landed, they saw a large crowd of people running to meet them. Did Jesus tell them to go away? No! He felt sorry for them and began to heal the sick people they had brought.

When it got late the disciples started to worry. "Jesus," they said, "These people must be hungry. Send them away so that they can buy food."

"Why don't *you* give them some food?" said Jesus.

"We could never buy enough bread to feed all these people!" replied Philip.

"Look!" said Andrew. "Here is a boy who is willing to share his lunch, but he has only five small loaves of bread and two small fish. That will never be enough!"

Jesus smiled and said, "Tell everyone to sit down on the grass."
Then he thanked God for the food and began to break the bread and fish into pieces.

The disciples passed around the food and everyone had plenty to eat. Can you count how many baskets of food were left over?

Wasn't it nice of the boy to share his lunch?
Jesus made his little lunch into a big dinner!

Peter Gets Wet

Matthew 14:22–33

It was night and Jesus was praying. All the people had gone home and the disciples were sailing across the lake. Can you see their boat far away?

In the middle of the night Jesus
decided to walk across the water to the
boat. But the disciples were afraid when they
saw him.

"Look," they cried, "a ghost is coming!"
"Don't be afraid!" said Jesus. "It's just me."

Peter still wasn't sure. "If it's you, Jesus, tell me to walk on top of the water too."

"Alright," said Jesus. So Peter got out of the boat.

At first Peter did just fine. But when he saw the wind and the waves, he was afraid and began to sink.

"Help me, Jesus!" he cried.

Jesus reached out and caught his hand. He helped Peter get back into the boat. "Why did you look at the waves instead of me?" he asked.

Who Am I?

Matthew 16:13–17; 17:1–9

One day Jesus asked his disciples, "Do you really know who I am?"

"Yes!" answered Peter. "You are God's Son!"

Six days later Jesus took Peter, James, and John to the top of a high mountain. Then he showed them what he would look like someday. His clothes and face shone brightly like the sun!

Two other men appeared and talked to him too. They were Moses and Elijah, men who had lived long ago.

Suddenly a cloud covered them up and they heard God say, "This is my Son! I love him and I'm happy with him! Be sure to listen to him!"

Peter, James, and John were afraid and fell to the ground. But Jesus touched them and said, "Don't be afraid!" When they looked up they saw that the bright light and the other men were gone. But they would never forget what they had seen!

A Boy Is Helped

Matthew 17:14–20
Mark 9:14–29

When Jesus and the three disciples came down from the mountain, they saw a large crowd. Some of the people were arguing loudly, but they all stopped when they saw Jesus.

"What are you arguing about?" he asked.

"My son is very sick," said one
of the men, "but your disciples
could not heal him. Please help him if you can!"

"If I can?" said Jesus. "Don't you believe I can make
him well?"

"Oh, yes!" said the boy's father, "I believe you!
Please help me when I have a hard time believing!"

So Jesus healed the
boy that very day.

Later his disciples said,
"Jesus, why couldn't we
heal the boy?"

"Because you do not
have very much faith in
God," he answered. "See
this tiny little mustard
seed? If you have only
this much faith, you will
be able to do great things
for God."

The Good Neighbor

Luke 10:25–37

One day someone asked Jesus a question. "The Bible tells us to love God with all our heart," he said, "and to love our neighbor. But who is my neighbor?"

In reply Jesus told this story:

A man was walking along a road. Suddenly, robbers jumped out from behind some bushes. They beat him and took his clothes.

The man lay on the road half-dead. He could not get up and could only moan, "Somebody please help me!"

Along came a priest. Would he help the poor man? No. He went to the other side of the road and walked on by.

Soon a Levite came by. "Help me, please!" cried the wounded man to the Levite.

Do you think he helped him? No, he did not. Away he went, leaving the poor man far behind.

Finally a Samaritan came by. He saw the man who was hurt and felt sorry for him. He put bandages on his cuts and bruises.

Then he put the wounded man on his donkey and took him to a nearby inn. He bought him food and a place to stay so he could rest and get well.

The next day he handed the innkeeper two silver coins. "Take care of the wounded man," he told him. "I will come back to check on him soon, and will pay you back if you have spent more money than this."

Then Jesus said, "Who was a good neighbor to the man who needed help? Was it the priest? Was it the Levite? Or was it the Samaritan?

"Yes! You are right! It was the Samaritan! Go now, and be a good neighbor to other people!"

One Is Thankful

Luke 17:11–19

Here come ten men who have leprosy. "Unclean! Unclean!" they cry, and everyone runs away.

The people are afraid of the lepers. They will not touch them or get close to them. They do not want to get sick with this terrible disease.

What a sad and lonely life the lepers live! They cannot stay with their families, so they live together outside the village.

One day Jesus came to their village. "Jesus! Please have pity on us!" shouted the lepers.

Jesus felt sorry for the ten men. "Go visit the priests and show them you are healed," he said.

The lepers believed Jesus and did what he said. As they walked along, their leprosy disappeared! All their sores were gone!

One leper saw that he was healed and began to praise God. He ran back and threw himself down at Jesus' feet to thank him.

Jesus said, "Didn't I heal ten men? Why are you the only one who came back to thank me?" Then he told the man to get up and go on his way.

"Your faith has healed you," he said.

Lost And Found

Luke 15

The teachers were upset with Jesus. "Look at that!" they muttered to each other. "Jesus is talking and eating with sinners! Doesn't he know what bad people they are?"

Then Jesus told three stories to show how much God loves each person, even when they disobey him.

Here is the first story:

This shepherd has a
hundred sheep. He is
counting them to be sure
they are all there. Uh-oh!
One is missing!

The shepherd leaves his
other sheep and goes to
look for his lost lamb.
"There you are!" he
cries at last.

The shepherd is
so happy that he
calls his friends and
neighbors to come
celebrate with him!

God is like the shepherd and we are like the lost
sheep. How happy God is to forgive us when we are
sorry for disobeying him!

This woman has ten coins. But when she counts them, she can find only nine.

So she lights a lamp and begins to sweep the house, looking carefully for the lost coin.

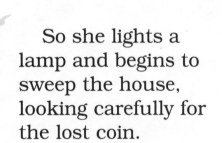

When she finds the missing coin she is so happy that she calls all her friends and neighbors to show them!

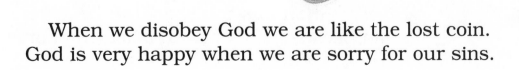

When we disobey God we are like the lost coin. God is very happy when we are sorry for our sins.

Here is the third story:

This man has two sons, but he is very sad because one of them is leaving home.

98

The young man goes to a city far away. He spends all his money with the wrong kind of friends.

Now he is hungry, but his friends have left and no one gives him any food. So he gets a job feeding pigs.

"The pigs have enough to eat and I do not," he says, looking hungrily at their food.

Finally the young man decides to return home to his father, where there is plenty to eat.

His father has been watching for him and sees him way off in the distance.

The father runs to meet his boy. He hugs and kisses him! "Bring new clothes for my son!" he tells his servants. "Put a ring on his finger and sandals on his feet! Quickly! Prepare some food so we can all celebrate and be glad!"

The other son was angry. "It isn't fair!" he said. "I stayed home and worked, but no one gave me a party!" And he went outside to pout.

His father found him and said, "Don't be angry! I will share everything I have with you. But we should all be happy because your brother was lost, and now he is found!"

Jesus Loves Children

Mark 10:13–16

One day some mothers and fathers brought their children to see Jesus.

But the disciples said, "Can't you see that Jesus is busy? He doesn't have time to bother with children!"

Jesus heard what they were saying and began to
scold his disciples. "Leave them alone!" he said. "Let
the children come to me! Don't you know that God
loves little children?"

Then he took the children into his arms.
He hugged them and blessed them.

Did you know that you can be blessed too?
Here is a blessing especially for you:

May God bless you and keep you safe,
May his light shine on your face,
May he give you peace and grace.

The Day Jesus Cried

John 11:1–44

One day a messenger from Bethany came running up to Jesus. "I have bad news for you," he panted. "Your friend Lazarus is very sick. His two sisters, Mary and Martha, sent me to tell you."

Two days later Jesus and his disciples began the journey to Bethany. When they arrived they found that Lazarus was already dead.

Many friends had come to comfort Mary and Martha because they had lost their brother.

When the sisters saw Jesus they said, "If only you had come sooner our brother would not have died!"

Jesus saw them weeping, and he began to cry too. "Take me to the tomb," he said.

Now Lazarus' tomb was a cave with a stone across the front. "Take away the stone!" commanded Jesus. Then after praying he said loudly, "Lazarus, come out!"

Out came Lazarus, wrapped in strips of cloth!
Everyone was so happy to see him alive!

Then Jesus made a wonderful promise: "Anyone
who believes in me, even if he dies, will someday
come back to life and never die again!"

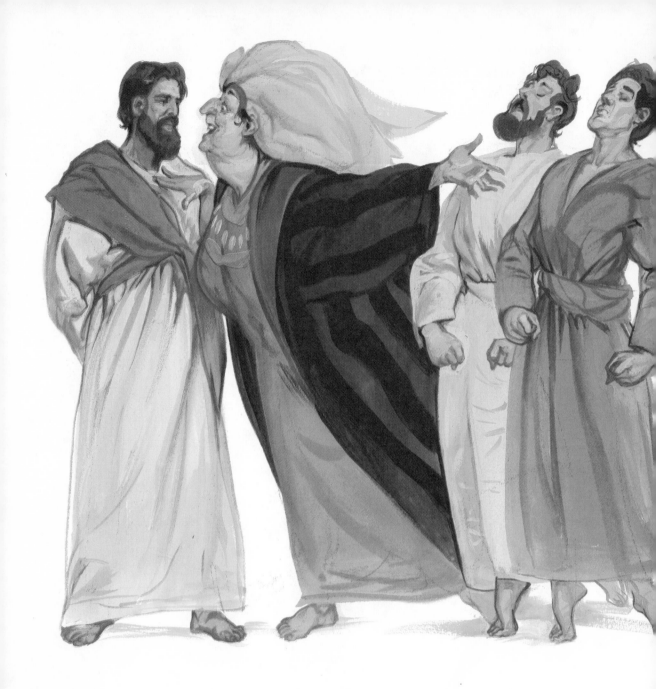

Me First!

Matthew 20:20–28

James and John came with their mother to see Jesus and to ask him a favor. "When you become a great king," they said, "we would like to sit next to your throne, one of us on each side of you."

But Jesus answered, "My Father has already decided who will sit there!"

The other disciples were angry with James and John.
"Well, imagine that!" said one.
"Who do they think they are!" complained another.
"They're no better than us!" grumbled a third.
You see, they all wanted to be first and to sit in the
best and most important seat.

Jesus heard them grumbling and murmuring, so he called them all together and taught them a lesson.

"If you want to be an important person in God's eyes, you must help other people and let them be first.

Can you think of someone you can help?

Little Man In A Tree

Luke 19:1–10

Zacchaeus was very short. If he wanted to reach something on a high shelf, he had to stand on a stool.

When Zacchaeus sat on a chair, his feet almost touched the floor—but not quite!

Guess which one is Zacchaeus!

But being short did not bother Zacchaeus. He could always find a way to get what he wanted, for he was very smart.

He had become quite wealthy as a tax collector, because he cheated people by charging them too much money.

One day Jesus came to town. Zacchaeus wanted to see Jesus, but he couldn't, for he was too short to see over the crowd.

"I won't let a few tall people keep me from seeing Jesus!" thought Zacchaeus. Quickly he ran ahead of the crowd and climbed up into a sycamore tree. "No one will see me up here!" he chuckled to himself.

Soon Jesus was right under the sycamore tree.
Zacchaeus was staring at him when suddenly, to his
surprise, Jesus looked straight up into his eyes.
"Zacchaeus!" he called. "Come down out of that
tree! I am going to visit your house today!"

"How did he know my name?" wondered Zacchaeus as he shimmied down the tree. But he was very happy to meet Jesus.

As he stood in front of Jesus, Zacchaeus didn't feel very smart anymore. "Lord," he said, "I'm going to give half of my money to help the poor, and if I have cheated someone, I will pay him back even more than I took."

Now that was a smart thing for Zacchaeus to say! Don't you think so?

A Blind
Man Sees

Mark 10:46–52

Bartimaeus sat on the hot,
dusty road that led out of Jericho.
He could not see the people go by,
for he was blind. But Bartimaeus
could hear them coming.

"Help a poor blind man!" he
would beg, and many kind people
gave him money.

One day a great crowd of people passed by. "What is going on?" asked Bartimaeus. When he found out that Jesus was passing by he began to shout loudly, "Jesus! Have pity on me!"

"Shhhh!" someone said. "You are making too much noise!" But Bartimaeus only shouted louder, "Jesus! Have pity on me!"

Jesus stopped walking and turned around. "Where is the man who is shouting?" he asked.

"Cheer up!" said the people to Bartimaeus. "Jesus wants to see you!"

Bartimaeus quickly jumped to his feet. "What is it you want?" asked Jesus kindly.

"Lord, I want to see," he replied.

"Because you believe in me, I will heal you," said Jesus.

Suddenly Bartimaeus could see, and do you know
what he saw? He was looking straight into the face of
Jesus! With a singing heart he joined the crowd and
followed Jesus down the road.

Jesus Rides
A Donkey

Luke 19:28–48

Jesus needed a donkey to ride into Jerusalem. "You will find one in the next village," he said. So two disciples ran ahead to look for it.

As they began to untie the donkey, some people asked, "What are you doing?"

"Jesus needs it," the disciples replied. "He will send it back soon." So the people let them take it.

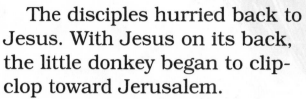

The disciples hurried back to Jesus. With Jesus on its back, the little donkey began to clip-clop toward Jerusalem.

"Jesus is going to be our King!" cried the people. They threw their coats, and branches from the trees, down on the road in front of him and began to shout,

"Hosanna! Hosanna! Blessed is our King!"

Soon they could see the city of Jerusalem. Its white buildings of stone stood proud and strong in the light of the setting sun.

Everyone else was excited but Jesus was sad.

"Oh, Jerusalem!" he cried. "I wish you would listen to me! But since you won't, your enemies will come and knock down your walls and proud buildings."

When they reached the temple, they found people buying and selling in the temple courtyard.

This made Jesus angry, so he overturned their tables and benches. "The temple is a place to come and pray," he said, "not a place to make money!"

The leaders and teachers were very unhappy with Jesus, but the people listened eagerly to what he said.

Two Small Coins

Mark 12:41–44

In the temple there was a treasure box where people put in money as an offering to God.

This man must be very rich. Look at all the money he is putting into the treasure box!

A poor widow came next. She pulled out two small coins, all the money she had. Clink! Clink! went the coins as she dropped them into the treasure box.

"See that poor widow?" said Jesus. "She gave more than the rich man. He gave money he didn't need, but she gave all that she had to God!"

Money
For Judas

Matthew 23:1–3; 26:3–16

Every day Jesus went to Jerusalem to teach. The people loved to hear him talk, but the leaders and the teachers did not like Jesus.

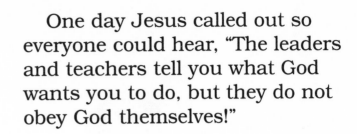

One day Jesus called out so everyone could hear, "The leaders and teachers tell you what God wants you to do, but they do not obey God themselves!"

After hearing this, the leaders of the people gathered together secretly. "We must find a way to get rid of Jesus," they said.

Judas, one of the twelve disciples, had been a friend of Jesus for a long time. He was in charge of the purse where money was kept for buying food. But sometimes he would steal money for his own use.

Judas went to the leaders of the people and asked, "How much money will you give me if I show you where you can find Jesus when he is alone?"

"We will give you thirty silver coins," they said.

Do you think Judas will help these evil men get rid of Jesus? He is not a very good friend if he loves money more than he loves Jesus, is he?

The Last Meal

John 13

Every spring, when flowers were blooming and birds were singing, people traveled to Jerusalem to celebrate the Feast of Passover. Jesus and his disciples got ready to eat the Passover meal too.

136

Before they ate, Jesus took a bowl of water and began to wash their dirty feet one by one.

"No, Jesus!" said Peter. "You shouldn't have to wash my feet!"

But Jesus replied, "I am doing this so you will learn to help each other, just as I am helping you."

Later, as they were eating, Jesus said, "One of you will hand me over to evil men who want to get rid of me."

"Who would do such a thing!" they all asked, but Judas got up and left the room.

Then Jesus told them, "Tonight you will all run away and leave me alone."

"I will never leave you!" exclaimed Peter.

"Yes, you will, Peter," Jesus replied. "When you hear a rooster crow, you will know that I was right."

Who do you think was right—Jesus or Peter?

The Garden

Matthew 26:36–75

After the Passover
meal, Jesus and his
disciples went to a
quiet garden called
Gethsemane.

"Come pray with me," said Jesus to Peter, James, and John as he led them farther into the garden. How sad and troubled he looked!

Then Jesus fell with his face to the ground, and began to pray to his Father in heaven.

Why do you think Jesus is so sad? Is it because he knows what will happen to him very soon?

When Jesus looked at Peter, James, and John, he found them fast asleep.

"Couldn't you stay awake to pray even for a little while?" he asked them.

But now it was too late. Already they could see an angry crowd approaching. Judas, one of the twelve disciples, was leading the way.

Judas came up to Jesus and kissed him so
that the crowd would know which one to grab.
Then all the disciples ran away, for they were
afraid. But Peter followed a little way behind.

The men took Jesus to the leaders of the people. They could find nothing wrong with Jesus, so they asked him, "Are you God's Son?"

"Yes, I am," he replied.

This made them very angry. "He must die!" they shouted. Then they hit him and spit in his face.

146

Peter waited outside to hear what would happen to Jesus.

"Aren't you a friend of Jesus?" a servant girl asked.

"No, I'm not!" said Peter. "I don't even know him!"

Just then a rooster crowed and Peter remembered what Jesus had told him. He hurried away and began to sob. He was sorry for what he had said!

The Sad Day

Mark 15; John 19: 38–42

Early the next morning, just as the sun came up,
the leaders took Jesus to see Pilate the governor.
Pilate asked him many questions, but Jesus would
not answer. Finally he asked, "Are you really a king?"

"Yes, I am," replied Jesus.

Then Pilate talked to the leaders. "This man has done nothing wrong!" he said. "Why do you want to kill him?"

But the leaders only shouted louder, "He must die!"

At last Pilate agreed to do as the leaders wished. Pilate's soldiers took Jesus away. They hit him and laughed at him. Then they made him carry a big, heavy wooden cross on his back.

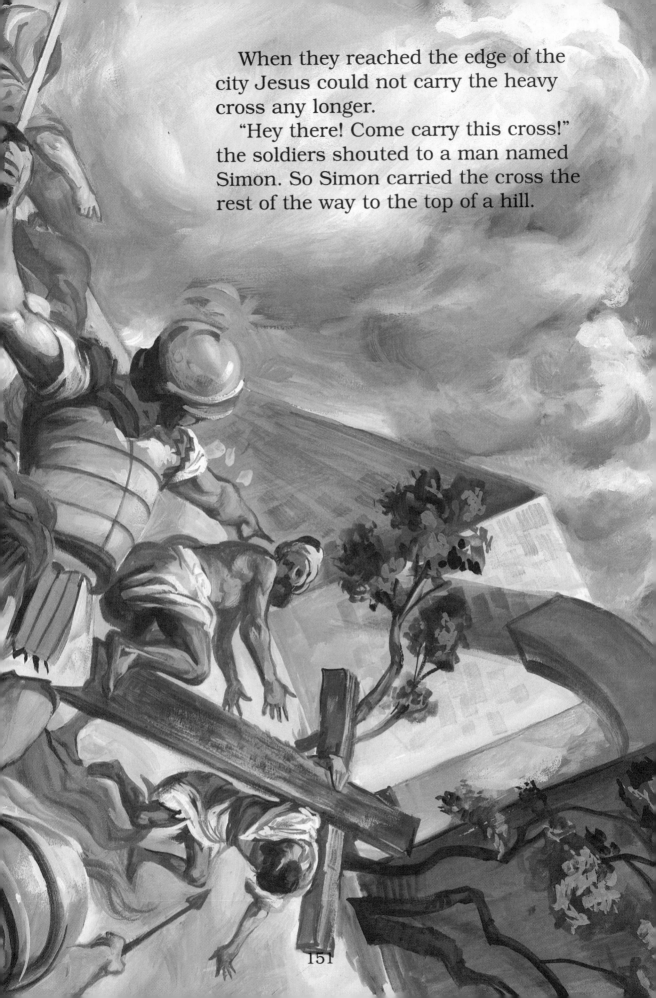

When they reached the edge of the
city Jesus could not carry the heavy
cross any longer.

"Hey there! Come carry this cross!"
the soldiers shouted to a man named
Simon. So Simon carried the cross the
rest of the way to the top of a hill.

The soldiers took Jesus and two men who were robbers, and nailed them each to a cross. Jesus' friends watched and cried from a distance.

When Jesus was dead, his friends took him down from the cross. They wrapped him in a clean cloth and put him in a tomb.

"We will never see Jesus again," they thought.

It was the saddest day that ever happened.

The Happy Day

Matthew 28:1–4
John 20:1–20

Very early on Sunday morning something happened
to Jesus' tomb. The ground began to shake, and a
bright angel appeared. Quick as a flash he rolled away
the heavy stone that was in front of the tomb.

Was Jesus inside? No, he wasn't!

A little while later Mary Magdalene came to the tomb. How surprised she was to find the heavy stone rolled away! She ran back immediately to tell Peter and John.

Peter and John ran as fast as they could to the tomb. Sure enough, the tomb was empty! Where was Jesus?

Peter and John left, but Mary stayed near the tomb crying. Suddenly she saw two angels inside the tomb.

"Why are you crying?" they asked.

"Because someone took Jesus away and I don't know where they put him," she sobbed.

Then Mary turned around and saw a man standing there. She thought he was the gardener.

"Did you take him away? Please tell me!" she pleaded.

The man said, "Mary!" Immediately she knew who he was.

It was Jesus! He was alive!

"Go tell the disciples that you have seen me!" said Jesus. But when Mary ran to tell them, they did not believe her.

That very night, when the disciples were together, Jesus suddenly appeared right in the middle of the room! The disciples could hardly believe their eyes. So it was true after all! Jesus was alive!

This was the happiest day that ever happened!

Jesus Says Goodbye

John 21:1–14
Acts 1:1–11

Jesus didn't stay with the disciples anymore. But every once in a while he would suddenly appear.

One morning, after the disciples had fished all night, Jesus appeared on the shore. "Didn't you catch any fish?" he called to them.

"No," they answered.

"Throw your nets in one more time," called Jesus.

When the disciples did this, they caught so many fish they could hardly pull the net to shore!

Then Jesus and the disciples talked together and had a nice breakfast of bread and fried fish.

The last time the disciples saw Jesus he told them he had a special job for them. "You must go all over the world and tell everyone the good news that I am alive! But don't start yet," he said. "Wait in Jerusalem until I send my Holy Spirit to help you!"

Then Jesus took them to the top of the Mount of Olives. As the disciples watched, Jesus began to go up in the air. Up, up, up he went until they could no longer see him!

Suddenly they noticed two men dressed in white
standing next to them. "Why are you looking up into
the sky?" they asked. "Jesus will come back down
from heaven someday the same way he just went up!"
Isn't it nice to know that Jesus is coming back?

The New Helper

Acts 2

After Jesus left, the disciples walked back to Jerusalem. They waited and prayed for the Helper that Jesus had promised.

Then one day it happened—they heard the roaring sound of a mighty wind!

Suddenly a flame of fire rested on each person, and they were all filled with God's Holy Spirit. The new Helper had come!

Other people heard the roaring wind too, and ran to see what it was. They found the disciples praising God in many different languages.

"I hear them talking in the language I speak at home," said each one in amazement.

Peter stood up and said, "Don't be so surprised! God promised many years ago to send us his Holy Spirit. Even though you killed his Son, Jesus, God brought him back to life!"

"What shall we do?" cried the people.

"You must feel sorry for your sins and believe in Jesus," replied Peter. "Then God will give you the Holy Spirit too."

Many of the people who heard Peter believed in Jesus. Every day they met together to share their food and to learn more about God. Now they were all part of a new family—God's family!

The Beggar Jumps

Acts 3:1–4:31

There was a man in Jerusalem who couldn't walk. So every day his friends carried him to the temple to beg for money.

One afternoon Peter and John came walking by. "Be kind to a poor beggar!" he called out to them.

Peter and John stopped. "Look at us!" said Peter. The beggar looked at them eagerly, expecting some money.

"I have no money," said Peter, "but I have something better!" He took the beggar by the hand and said, "Jesus makes you well. Get up and walk!"

Right away the beggar jumped up. "Look!" he cried happily. "I can walk!"

The people all stared at him in surprise.

Then Peter began to tell everyone about Jesus. "We didn't make this man well," he said. "Jesus did! Jesus is God's Son and he is alive!"

But the leaders and temple guards didn't like what Peter said. They took Peter and John and put them in prison.

The next day the leaders let Peter and John go.
"Stop telling people about Jesus!" they said.

Did Peter and John stop telling people about Jesus?
No! They talked about him even more! They weren't
afraid, because the Holy Spirit was helping them.

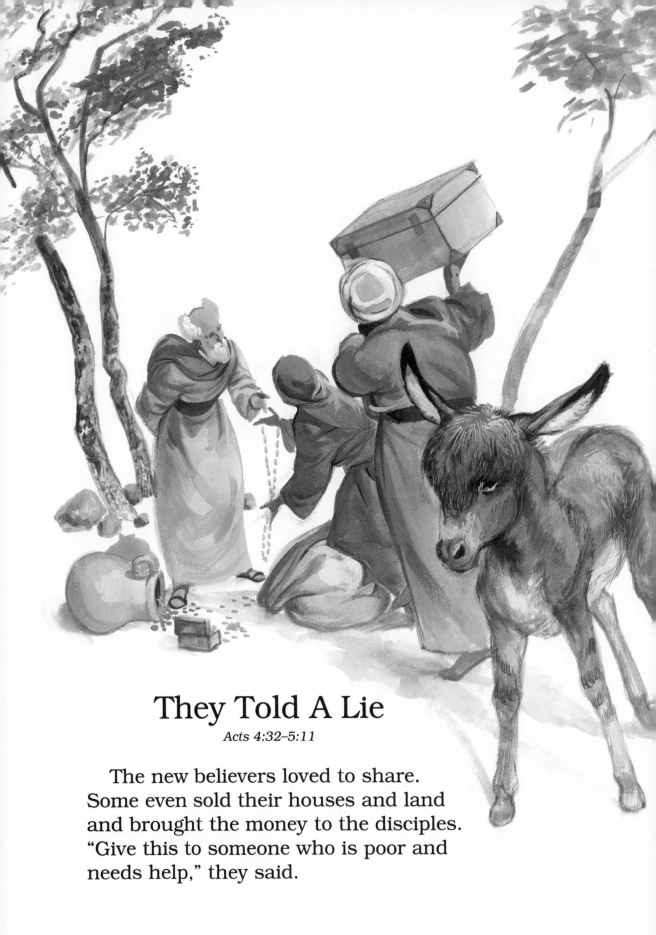

They Told A Lie

Acts 4:32–5:11

The new believers loved to share.
Some even sold their houses and land
and brought the money to the disciples.
"Give this to someone who is poor and
needs help," they said.

One day a man named Ananias and his wife, Sapphira, sold a field. "Let's give some of the money to the disciples," said Ananias, "and tell them we gave it all. No one will ever know the difference!"

Sapphira agreed.

Then Ananias went to see Peter. "I sold my field,"
he said, "and this is how much money I received."

But Peter replied, "Do what you want with your
money, Ananias, but don't lie to God about it!"

When Ananias heard this, he fell right down and
died. Some young men carried him out and buried him.

A little while later Sapphira came into the room.

"Did you sell your field for this much money?" Peter asked her.

"Yes," she replied.

"Why did you and Ananias agree to lie?" asked Peter. "The young men who buried him will bury you too."

Immediately Sapphira fell down and died. Then all the believers knew how important it was to tell the truth!

A Ride In The Chariot

Acts 8:26–40

One day God told Philip, one of the twelve disciples, to go to the desert. Right away Philip obeyed. Along the way he met a man from Ethiopia who was sitting in his chariot reading.

"I see you are reading the Bible," said Philip. "Do you understand what it says?"

"No," answered the Ethiopian. "Come, ride with me and tell me what it means."

So Philip told him about Jesus.

Soon they passed some water. "I want to be baptized!" said the Ethiopian. They stopped the chariot and Philip baptized him.

Then suddenly Philip disappeared! God took him away so he could tell other people about Jesus. But even though Philip was gone, the Ethiopian was not alone. God's Helper, the Holy Spirit, would always be with him!

The Light On The Road

Acts 9:1–25

There was one man who hated Jesus. His name was Saul.
Saul looked everywhere for people who loved Jesus. Then
he took them away from their families and put them in
prison. Saul did not want anyone to believe that Jesus was
God's Son.

One day Saul and some friends went to Damascus. He was looking for more people to put into prison.

Suddenly a light from heaven, brighter than the sun, flashed around them, and everyone fell to the ground! Saul heard a voice that said, "Saul, Saul, why are you trying to hurt me?"

"Who are you?" asked Saul.

"I am Jesus," replied the voice. "When you hurt my disciples, you are really hurting me. Now stand up! I have a special job for you. From now on you must tell people about me!"

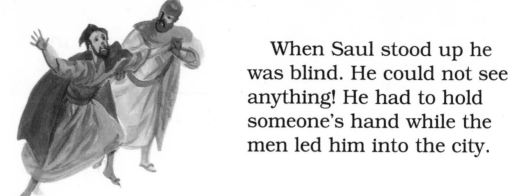

When Saul stood up he was blind. He could not see anything! He had to hold someone's hand while the men led him into the city.

After three days a good man named Ananias came to visit Saul. "Jesus sent me," said Ananias. "He wants you to see again, and he wants to give you his Holy Spirit." Ananias put his hands on Saul's eyes.

Immediately Saul could see the beautiful world again! He was glad to have God's Holy Spirit helping him as he began to tell people about Jesus!

But some of the people were not pleased. "We must find a way to stop him," they said. Day and night they watched the city gate so that they could catch him.

Finally one night Saul's friends put him in a basket. They lowered him down over the city wall and away he went to Jerusalem to meet with the other believers.

The Widows' Friend

Acts 9:36–42

Dorcas was a kind woman who loved Jesus. Here she sits with her needle and thread. What do you suppose she is sewing?

She is making clothes for widows and their children because they have no father to take care of them. See how much the children and their mothers love Dorcas!

One day Dorcas got
sick. She did not get well,
and soon she died. Her
friends were very sad.

Then they heard that
Peter was nearby. "Please
come at once!" they
begged him.

When they took
Peter to Dorcas' room,
the widows stood
around him weeping.
"See the beautiful
clothes she made for
us!" they cried.

Peter asked everyone to leave the room. Then after he had prayed he said, "Dorcas, get up!" Dorcas opened her eyes and sat up!

"You can come in now," called Peter to the others. What hugs and laughter filled the room!

Many people believed in Jesus when they heard about Dorcas.

God Loves Everybody

Acts 10

Cornelius lived in the city of Caesarea. He was a soldier from a faraway land, and was in charge of a hundred other soldiers. "Do this!" he would say, and they would do it at once.

One afternoon while he was praying, Cornelius saw an angel. "Send for a man named Peter," said the angel. "He has a message from God for you."

So Cornelius sent three men to look for Peter.

The three men went to Joppa and found the house
where Peter was staying. "What do you want?" asked
Peter.

The men told Peter about Cornelius and the angel.
"Will you come with us?" they asked.

"Yes, I will," replied Peter.

When Peter met Cornelius he said, "Our law says
we must not visit with people from other countries.
But God told me that he loves everyone, so that is
why I came."

Cornelius and his friends listened eagerly as Peter told them about Jesus. As he talked they were filled with the Holy Spirit and began to praise God.

"This shows that God loves everyone!" exclaimed Peter. "He will give his Holy Spirit to anyone who believes in him!"

Peter And The Angel

Acts 12:1–19

King Herod put some of the believers in prison.
When he saw that this made the leaders happy, he
put Peter in prison too. Sixteen soldiers guarded him
carefully so he could not escape.

One night while Peter was sleeping, an angel appeared in the prison. The angel shook Peter and said, "Quick, get up and follow me!"

Peter's chains fell off and he followed the angel out into the city. Then the angel disappeared.

Peter went at once to a friend's house and knocked on the door. "Who is it?" asked Rhoda the servant girl.

"This is Peter!" he replied.

Rhoda ran to tell the others. She was so happy that she forgot to open the door!

At first Peter's friends did not believe Rhoda. But when they finally opened the door, they saw that it really was Peter. God had answered their prayers!

A Long Journey
Acts 13, 14

The church in Antioch had many believers. "It is time to start a church somewhere else," said the Holy Spirit. So they sent Barnabas and Paul to start new churches. Paul's real name was Saul, but everyone called him Paul.

Paul and Barnabas got on a ship and sailed to other countries. Then they walked from town to town telling people about Jesus.

These people don't look like they want to hear about Jesus, do they? No! They chased Paul and Barnabas out of their town.

But some people were happy to hear about Jesus!
Finally Paul and Barnabas went back to Antioch.
They were glad that they had obeyed the Holy Spirit,
for now there were many new churches.

It Happened In Philippi

Acts 15:36–41; 16:9–40

After quite a long time, Paul decided to go back and visit the churches he had started. He took a man named Silas and walked from one church to another. Then God told them to sail to the city of Philippi.

In Philippi they met a very kind lady named Lydia
who sold purple cloth.

"Please," she begged, "come and stay at my house!"
So they did.

Then one day some men became angry with Paul
and Silas for doing miracles and teaching about Jesus.
"These men are troublemakers," they told the governor.
"Whip them and throw them in prison!" he ordered.

Did Paul and Silas complain? No! They sang songs
and prayed while the other prisoners listened.

Suddenly, in the middle of the night, the ground began to shake. The doors of the prison flew open, and everyone's chains fell off!

The jailer knew that God must have done this. He fell on his knees and cried, "What must I do to be saved?"

"Believe in Jesus," answered Paul and Silas.

The jailer and all his family believed in Jesus that very night!

Two Cities

Acts 17:16–18:11

The city of Athens was full of idols. Some were made of gold, some of silver, and some of stone. The people of Athens bowed down and worshiped the idols.

When Paul came to Athens he was sad to see all the idols. "Why do you worship a statue that cannot move?" he asked. "God is alive! You should worship him!"

A few people listened to Paul, but most of them didn't.

Paul left Athens and went to the city of Corinth. Can you guess what he did there? He made tents with his friends Priscilla and Aquila. But he also told everyone he could about Jesus, and this time many people listened.

Paul In Prison

Acts 21:3–26:32

"Don't go to Jerusalem!" the believers begged Paul. "You will get into trouble if you go there!"

But Paul would not listen. "I must go where the Holy Spirit tells me to go," he said.

So the believers knelt down and prayed for Paul.

Sure enough, while Paul was worshiping at the temple in Jerusalem, some people recognized him. They grabbed him and yelled, "Men, come help us! This is the man who is trying to change our rules!"

The people began to beat Paul. They wanted to kill him! But just then some soldiers ran up and stopped the angry crowd. The soldiers took Paul and put him in prison.

Paul stayed in prison for a long time. Finally the governor decided to put him on a ship and send him far away to Rome.

Paul was glad that God would be with him wherever he went, even as far away as Rome.

The Shipwreck

Acts 27, 28

Paul was on his way to Rome. At first it was sunny and warm, but then a cold wind began to blow.

"Winter is almost here," warned Paul. "Don't go any further." But the captain of the ship wouldn't listen.

Before long a terrible storm began. For many days the wind drove the ship here and there. No one could see the sun.

"We will all die!" cried the men.

But Paul said, "No one will die!"

The ship hit bottom near an island and became stuck in the sand. Everyone jumped into the water and swam to shore. Not a single person was lost!

The people on the island welcomed them kindly and built a fire so that they could get warm.

After winter Paul and the soldiers sailed on. How glad they were to finally reach Rome! The soldiers let Paul live in his own house. He told every visitor who came about Jesus.

May God be with you

Paul wrote many letters to his friends in the churches. Someone else would write down what Paul wanted to say, and then he would finish the letter himself.

"May God be with you," he would write in big letters.

Heaven Is Our Home

Revelation 21, 22
Isaiah 11:6–9

Someday Jesus will come back.
He will take everyone who loves
and believes in him to heaven.

Heaven will be a happy place to live. There won't
be any more crying. No one will ever get hurt or die.

Heaven will be a bright place to live. There won't be any more night. It will always be day because God will be there, shining like the sun.

Heaven will be a joyful place to live. All the animals
and the children will play together happily!

Jesus says, "I am coming soon."
And we answer, "Yes, Jesus, please come soon!"